TORTURED EYES LEAD TORTURED LIVES

A SERIES OF WORKS DOCUMENTING

THE BULLSHIT WE GO THROUGH

BY: BEAKO!

TORTURED EYES LEAD
TORTURED LIVES
A SERIES OF
WORKS DOCUMENTING
THE BULLSHIT WE
GO THROUGH
BEAKO!
21

"TWEEKY BIRD REALIZED SHE HAD GONE TOO FAR, BUT BY NOW IT WAS FAR TOO LATE."

SELF-DESTRUCT

At what point does one admit that they are in dire need of assistance?

That a car wreck has occurred and that they have no first aid kit training

When does one finally admit that they caused the crash in the first place?

I stood in the road, waited for the right moment to jump, I caused it.

The swerve, the crunch of metal, and I poured gasoline on it afterwards

I realized I had gone too far, but by then it was already

far, far too late, so I doubled and tripled down and kept digging my grave

At what point does one admit their life is a car wreck gone up in flames?

"I LEARNED THAT A DOG'S LOVE IS UNCONDITIONAL,

WHEN I FELL IN PUPPY LOVE WITH YOU."

KICKED PUPPY

I love you, I'm just like a puppy
When you call my name I
Can feel my heart wagging and you see
There's much love in my eyes
Because I'm just like a puppy dog
I am obsessed with you
With pleasing you, being your lapdog
Tell me what do I do?
I won't make plans without your so-say
Sit happy in my cage
I wouldn't do it any other way
Won't grow to a new stage
Or even think until you command

Please don't abandon me
I can see you losing interest
Please don't abandon me
I can see you losing interest
Please don't abandon me
I can see you losing interest
Please don't abandon me
I can see you losing interest
Please don't abandon me
I can see you losing interest
Please don't abandon me
I can see you losing interest
Please don't abandon me
I can see you losing interest

"BUT PUPPIES GET KICKED AND LEFT ON THE STREET,
THAT'S WHERE THEY LEARN TO BARE THEIR TEETH."

KICKED PUPPY II

I loved you, where'd you go?
I'm much older now, colder, angrier
I feel bad lashing out
But I must admit it's the damage
From being left alone
I never really understood
What that was all about
Like why? Did you not like your puppy?
I jumped right off the peak of Everest
Just because I trusted you not to test
How much of an idiot I'd be
For you, if you asked me

"I'M TRYING SO HARD, I'M SO HUNGRY.

WHAT'S IT GONNA TAKE? TO ESCAPE THIS HELL?"

DISORDER

Am I not trying hard enough?

Everyone else is just fine, has

No problem filling their belly

I can't bring myself to do it

Fuck. Why do I have such a tough

Time being normal? Everybody

Else can bring themselves to do it

Just fine.

Just fine.

Just.

Fine.

Why?

am I?

Not

Like them?

"WHEN YOU'RE SO SMALL, SO INNOCENT,

YOU HAVE NO CHOICE BUT TO TRUST

THOSE MEANT TO CARE FOR YOU

AND YET,

IT'S STILL MY FAULT FOR HAVING

TRUSTED YOU."

FAMILY TIES

Trust.

1a : assured reliance on the character,

ability,

the strength,

or truth

of someone

or something.

b : one in which confidence is placed... Because of

You, I did not

learn the

meaning

Of this word

For a long

Long time

Fuck you

For that

"WHEN YOU KEEP PEOPLE OUT FOR SO LONG

YOU BUILD THIS ARMOR THAT FITS YOUR BODY SO WELL

YOU FORGET HOW TO LET THEM

BACK IN AGAIN."

WEARING ARMOR TO SLEEP

When you keep people out for so long it becomes
Impossible to let them back in again
Everything is an attack, and every word drums
Over and over, overthinking again
Three meanings for each thing you will say to me and
None of them are what you actually mean
Eventually I will start to avoid you
Because it will surely someday become
Far, far too much for me, and it might start to mean
Taking off this armor to keep together
And baby, I wear this armor even to sleep

**"AND JUST WHO DO YOU THINK YOU ARE?
TO CLAIM ME AS YOURS, TAKE FROM MY BODY
AND STILL ASK ME TO DANCE FOR YOU?"**

MY BODY

Violation
Says my name in
Desperation
These hands
I do not want
Touching my shell
Audacity
Quite the
Audacity
To be touching
My body man
To take
And to demand
That I then dance
To entertain
Your friends
Fuck you
Fuck you
Fuck you
Human

**"SOMETIMES YOU GIVE IT YOUR BEST TRY.
REALLY, I MEAN REALLY PUT YOUR BACK INTO IT,
AND STILL
IT ALL FALLS APART JUST THE SAME.**

FUCK."

NOT ENOUGH

I did my best
I deserve some
Recognition
Here man, I gave
It my best shot

I did my best
And didn't become
what I wanted
Really? I
Gave it my best

What the fuck?

"I'm doing everything I can
To make it through
The darkness.
I know
That there is still light
Inside of me,
I'M GONNA
FIND IT AND
MAKE IT
FUCKING SHINE
IN ALL THE
DARK PLACES"

GROWTH

Growing is hard
It takes
Up a lot of
Time and
Care to see some
Progress
A sprouting bud
is still
More than it was
as a
Empty barren
Clay pot.
Growing is hard
It takes
Up a lot of
Time and
Care, however
To not
Try to grow is
Harder

"THESE CHAINS MAY HOLD ME BACK BUT I WON'T LET THEM STOP ME."

CHAINED BRAINS

It is ironic
How few people are willing to admit
That
These chains are holding
Me back from flying directly into
The
Sun
They say something like
"Bad idea, Icarus flew there once.."
But
I
Bet
That I can still fly
Higher than these fuckers have ever seen

"AND I'M GONNA LAUGH THROUGH THE PAIN,
MAKE LIFE MY BITCH, SHOW NO WEAKNESS.

BUT INSIDE I CANNOT BRING MYSELF
TO LAUGH
OR EVEN CRY."

FAKE IT 'TIL YOU MAKE IT

A short excerpt from a Certain Phone Call that will stick with me forever.

"And so, that's all
That's it, I'm not
Exactly
So happy
But I'm
Not sad
Not truly
I guess we'll
Have to see where
All of this goes

Any way that it pans out, I'm sure I'll tell you all about it later, I guess.
See ya."

MAY WE ALL HEAL

FROM THE THINGS

WE DO NOT TALK ABOUT.

<3